A MAGICAL MENAGERIE

A MAGICAL MENAGERIE

Tales from Perrault, Andersen, La Fontaine and Grimm

Retold by Sheila Wainwright
Illustrated by Francis Wainwright

1991

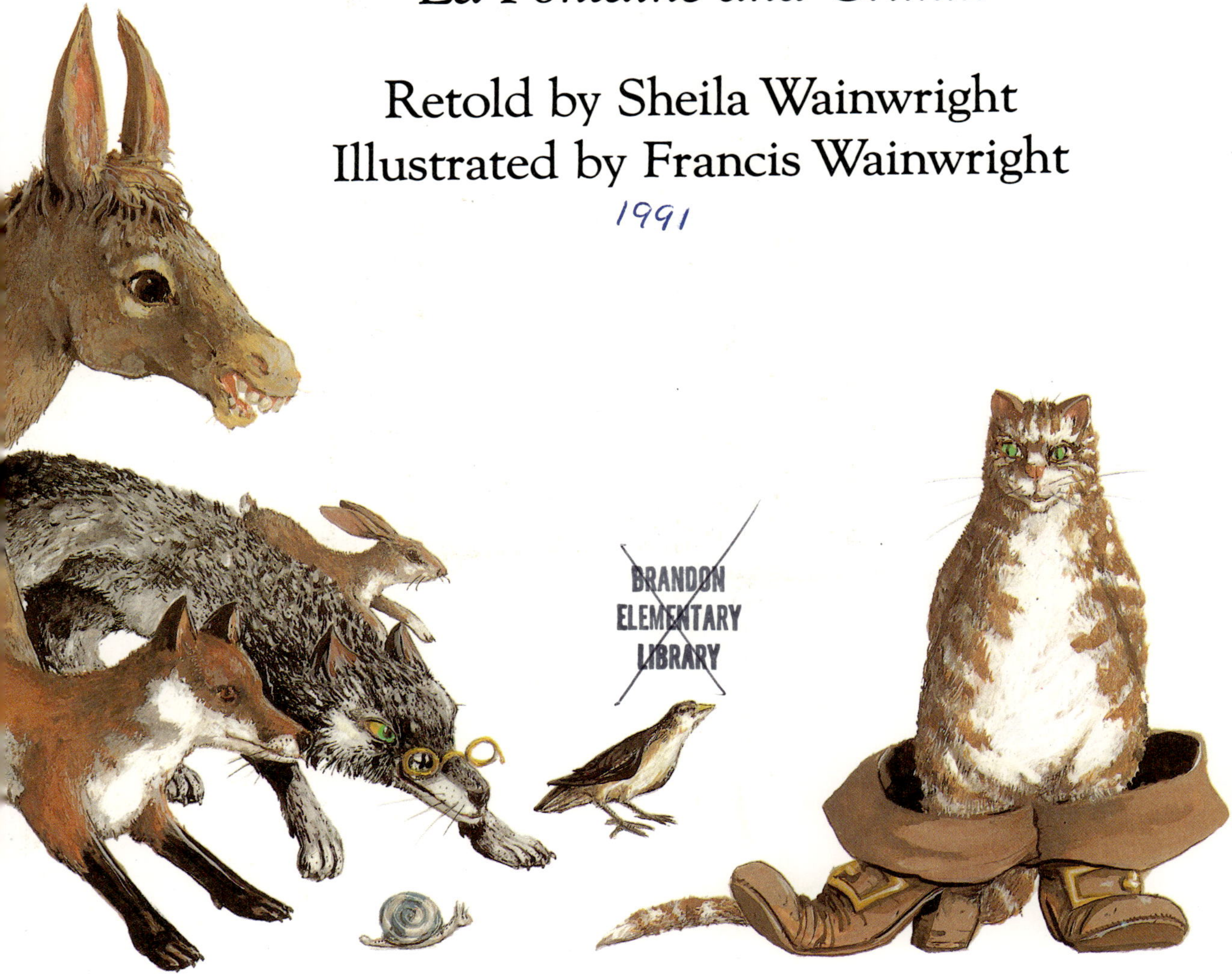

Henry Holt and Company · New York

Published in the United States by
Henry Holt and Company, Inc., 115 West 18th Street,
New York, New York 10011.
Originally published in Great Britain.

Library of Congress Cataloging in Publication Data is available.
Library of Congress Catalog Card Number: 88-45162

ISBN 0-8050-0888-8

First American Edition

Designer: Zena Flax
Printed in Hong Kong by South China Printing Co.
10 9 8 7 6 5 4 3 2 1

ISBN 0-8050-0888-8

Contents

"We will not touch a morsel, no, not even the leg of a fly, though we should die of starvation, until that disrespectful bruin has been punished for his insults."

from *The Tom-Tit and the Bear*

Charles Perrault 1628–1703

Born in Paris, France, Charles Perrault was the son of a barrister. He is remembered today for his famous collection of fairy-tales first published under the name of his son Pierre, and entitled *Histoires et contes du temps passé* (1697). These charming tales were based on French popular tradition.

Puss in Boots

There was once a poor miller who lived with his three sons, a donkey and a cat. When the miller died, the eldest son took the mill for himself, gave the middle son the donkey, and to the youngest of the three, he gave the cat.

The youngest son felt that his father's property had been divided very unfairly. "My two elder brothers can go into business together, using the donkey to help work the mill. Whereas I can do nothing with a cat, and will remain poor for the rest of my life."

"Don't despair, my good master," said the cat. "Provide me with a sack and a pair of well-fitting boots, and you will soon see that you have had a better bargain than either of your brothers."

The boy was so surprised to hear the cat talk, that he ran all the way to the shoemaker, and ordered a fine pair of boots in the softest leather. They were a perfect fit.

"I shall call you Puss in Boots!" said the boy, and handed him the sack he had asked for.

Puss in Boots then put some bran and lettuce into the sack and, with a cheerful wave to his master, set off in the direction of the woods to hunt rabbits. He stretched himself out on the grass with the sack at his side, and pretended to be dead. Before long, a young rabbit appeared, sniffed all round the sack, found the opening and crawled inside. "Got you!" cried Puss, and he pulled the drawstring tightly round the top of the sack. The plan was working beautifully. Without delay, he slung the sack over his shoulder and made his way to the King's palace.

The royal footmen were so amazed at the sight of a cat wearing boots that they escorted him to the throne room and presented him to the King. "Sire," said Puss, bowing low. "I have been sent by my noble lord, the Marquis of Carabas, to present Your Majesty with this gift of a young plump rabbit."

The King had never heard of the Marquis of Carabas, which was not surprising as it was a title that Puss in Boots had just invented for the miller's son, but he graciously accepted the rabbit.

Some days later, Puss caught a brace of pheasant in his sack and returned to the palace to offer them as another gift from his master, the Marquis of Carabas. The King accepted the pheasant and commanded Puss to thank his noble lord, and to pass by the royal kitchens for a dish of cream before going home.

As Puss in Boots left the palace, he overheard a group of courtiers discussing the arrangements for His Majesty's drive along the river with his daughter. Now the King's daughter was said to be the most beautiful princess in the whole world. Such an event as this was exactly what Puss in Boots had hoped for! In great haste, he ran back to his young master and said: "You will have riches beyond your wildest dreams if you will follow my instructions. All you have to do is go bathing in the river at the exact time and in the exact spot that I tell you. Leave the rest to me."

The strange request puzzled the miller's son, but as it was a warm day, he decided that a swim in the river was an excellent idea. They reached the appointed spot along the riverbank and the boy jumped into the cool, clear water. Crafty as ever, Puss in Boots quickly hid his master's clothes under a rock and took up his position at the roadside to keep watch. As Puss in Boots heard the sound of carriage wheels in the distance, he began waving frantically and crying out. "Help! Help! Someone please help! The Marquis of Carabas is drowning."

No sooner had the King heard this name, than he commanded his footmen to rescue the Marquis of Carabas.

While the miller's son was being dragged out of the river, Puss in Boots told the King that his noble master's clothes had been stolen by thieves while he was bathing. At once, the King ordered one of his men to return in haste to the palace and fetch a royal suit of clothes for the Marquis of Carabas to wear.

The Princess, alarmed at the noise and confusion, asked what was going on.

"Patience, my dear, and you shall see," said the King.

At length, the miller's son emerged from behind a bush. Dressed in such fine clothes, he was transformed into a handsome nobleman, and the Princess immediately fell in love. She persuaded the King, who was also greatly impressed by this handsome young Marquis, to invite him to accompany them on their drive.

Puss in Boots, who had observed all this with the greatest satisfaction, hurried off ahead of the royal carriage. On his way, he came across some simple peasants working in a meadow and said to them, "His Majesty the King will be driving past soon. When he stops and enquires as to who is the owner of this meadow, you will be wise to say that it belongs to the Marquis of Carabas – for if you say otherwise, you shall all have your heads chopped off!" The simple peasants were terrified to hear these threatening words.

A few minutes later, the royal carriage drove by. Sure enough, the King ordered his coachman to stop. "Tell me," asked the King, "who owns this fine meadow?"

"It belongs to the Marquis of Carabas, your Majesty," replied the frightened peasants. The King congratulated the miller's son on his fertile meadow and ordered the carriage to proceed.

Meanwhile, Puss had run further on along the road until he came across a ripe cornfield where some reapers were busy harvesting the corn. He repeated the same threatening words as before and when the King passed by a moment later, stopping to admire the rich grain and enquire as to who was the owner of this land, the terrified reapers chorused obediently, "The Marquis of Carabas!"

"Excellent!" said the King, "I never saw a finer crop."

The royal carriage drove on through the lush countryside and each time it stopped, the King was told the same story. The road twisted and turned until in the distance, there appeared a beautiful castle.

Puss in Boots had already reached the castle and gained entry by telling the gate-keeper that he brought an urgent message from his noble master. Now the castle belonged to a wicked ogre who possessed magic powers. It was he who really owned all the rich land that the King had been riding through.

Puss was quickly escorted to a great hall hung with animal skins and sinister looking weapons. There sat the ogre, as big as he was ugly. "Speak!" growled the ogre, "before I chew you into little pieces!"

"I have heard that you have the power to turn yourself into whatever you like," said Puss. "A lion, for instance, or any other wild animal. Can this be possible?"

"Indeed it can!" said the ogre proudly, and without more ado, transformed himself into a fierce lion. The lion let out such a roar

that Puss leapt out of the window. He waited outside until all went quiet, then cautiously leapt back on the window ledge to peep through. The lion had vanished. Only the ogre sat there, laughing loudly at the fright he had given his visitor. Puss jumped down and said, cunningly:

"That was real magic! But I'll wager that you would find it much more difficult turning yourself into a mouse!"

The ogre scoffed, "Difficult, did you say? Then watch this!" In a flash, the ogre disappeared and a little fieldmouse scampered across the floor. With one mighty pounce Puss caught the mouse and ate him up.

Now there was not a moment to lose. Puss told the servants that the ogre was dead and that their new master, the Marquis of Carabas, was to arrive at any moment with His Majesty the King.

As the King's carriage approached, the King, turning to the miller's son who sat by his side in silent confusion said, "So this is your country seat, is it? Sly dog, all this time not saying a word when we were wondering whose fine castle this could be!"

Puss quickly drew his young master to one side and explained all that had happened.

"You were right, my good friend," said the Marquis of Carabas. "I did have a better bargain than either of my brothers!"

It was obvious to the King that his daughter and the Marquis of Carabas had fallen in love. He gave his royal blessing on their marriage which took place soon afterwards.

The Marquis's two elder brothers were each given a small country estate. And Puss in Boots? His loyalty and quick thinking were rewarded with a suit of fine clothes, and the remarkable title of:

MOUSE-CATCHER EXTRAORDINARY TO THE MARQUIS OF CARABAS

Little Red Riding Hood and the Wolf

A pretty little girl lived in a quiet village on the edge of a forest. Her mother had made her a bright red hood, which suited her so well that everyone in the village called her Little Red Riding Hood.

One day, her mother said to her, "My dear, I would like you to go and visit your grandmother and take her this cake and a pot of jam. She has not been feeling well and a visit from you will cheer her up."

So Little Red Riding Hood prepared her basket, feeling very proud to be entrusted with this important errand. She promised not to stray from the path, or talk to any strangers, and with a cheerful wave, set off for her grandmother's cottage which was in a nearby village on the other side of the forest.

After walking for a while, she decided to take a rest and sat down on a tree stump. "I'll pick some wild flowers for grandmother," thought Little Red Riding Hood, and as she knelt down by a clump of bluebells, she heard a rustling sound.

"Who's there?" she called, turning quickly. There was a stirring in the bushes and then a large, grey wolf appeared.

"Good morning, dear child," said the wolf. "What a very pretty hood you're wearing."

Little Red Riding Hood was so astonished that she forgot her mother's warning and answered, "Thank you kindly. My mother made it for me."

"I see," said the cunning wolf, "and is your mother somewhere nearby, dear child? I should like to congratulate her on her handiwork."

"Oh no," said Little Red Riding Hood. "I have been given a special errand to take a cake and some jam to my grandmother who lives on the other side of the forest."

"Well, I declare!" said the wolf slyly. "What a good and responsible child you are. Does your grandmother live alone?"

"She does," replied Red Riding Hood, "in the prettiest black and white cottage with yellow roses round the door. She has not been well lately and I am going to cheer her up." With that, she placed her flowers in the basket and started on her way along the forest path.

The evil wolf licked his lips and thought, "You have certainly cheered me up too, you tasty little red-hooded creature! Your sweet self and your sick grandmother will provide me with food for the next few days!" He set off at a gallop, taking a short cut through the forest and, on reaching the village, wasted no time in finding the black and white cottage with yellow roses round the door. He knocked.

"Who's there?" came a frail sounding voice from inside.

"It is I, Little Red Riding Hood," said the wolf, trying to imitate the child. "I have brought you a cake and a pot of jam sent from my mother."

"Lift the latch, my dear, and let yourself in!" called the old lady.

Within seconds, the hungry wolf had opened the door, leapt on to the grandmother's bed and in a few greedy swallows, gobbled her up – nightgown and all. Only her spectacles and nightcap remained on the bed which the wolf quickly seized and put on. He then drew the curtains and climbed under the bed covers.

Eventually, Little Red Riding Hood arrived with her basket at the cottage door. She knocked and listened.

"Who is there?" called the wolf.

Little Red Riding Hood was rather startled by the unusual tone of her grandmother's voice, but replied, "It is I, Granny dear, I've

brought you one of your favourite cakes my mother has baked for you, and a pot of her home-made jam, and I've picked a lovely bunch of wild flowers for you."

The wolf pulled the bedclothes tightly under his chin and called in a soft voice, "Lift the latch, my dear, and come right in."

She did as she was told but, suddenly feeling that something was amiss, hesitated by the door. "I can't see you Granny. It's so dark in here!" she called, slightly alarmed.

"I have a headache," came the reply, "and the light bothers my eyes. Put your basket on the table and come and sit next to me."

Little Red Riding Hood was just about to bend over to give her grandmother a kiss, when she drew back exclaiming; "Granny, what big ears you have!"

"All the better to hear you with, my dear," came the reply.

Red Riding Hood strained her eyes and peered anxiously at the face staring back at her. "Oh Granny! Your eyes!" she gasped, "How big they look!"

The hoarse voice replied, "All the better to see you with, my dear." By now, Little Red Riding Hood could see large sharp teeth. She was frightened.

"Granny," she cried, "what big teeth you have!"

"ALL THE BETTER TO EAT YOU WITH, MY DEAR!"

A passing woodcutter, hearing Red Riding Hood's scream, ran into the cottage. With one mighty blow from his axe, he felled the wicked wolf. Then he wrapped Red Riding Hood in a blanket and sat her in a comfortable armchair. As she sobbed out her story, the dead wolf's bulging stomach began to move. In an instant, the woodcutter cut open the skin and out tumbled grandmother, none the worse for her frightening experience.

"That's the last we'll see of this monster," said the woodcutter, throwing the wolf's carcass over his shoulder. "The forest will be a much safer place now."

Donkey Skin

There was once a good, kind king who was loved and respected by his people. His kingdom prospered and he had no enemies. His queen was gentle and good-natured, and their only daughter was considered by all to be a most beautiful and charming girl. In fact, the king believed that he was the happiest man in the world.

In the royal stables, the king had a most unusual donkey. Every morning, amongst the donkey's straw bedding there appeared a large quantity of shiny gold pieces. Over the years, this amounted to a very large fortune, enabling the Imperial family to live in great luxury.

There came a time, however, when good fortune smiled no longer on the king. The queen became ill and was close to death. Broken-hearted, the king sat weeping at her bedside.

"My dear husband," she whispered, "You must promise me one thing before I die. Our daughter is still very young and I am worried that when the time comes for her to marry, she may be pursued by those who seek her fortune. Promise me now, that you will only agree to marry her to someone who truly loves her, someone who would die of sorrow if he could not marry her."

"I promise," said the king, and the queen died peacefully.

Now there was a sly and deceitful knight amongst the courtiers who overheard the queen's last words. He began to plot how he could marry the young princess and take possession of her fortune. First he tried wooing her with gifts, but the princess refused them all, for she did not trust him. Then, he took to his bed, pretending to be stricken with a fever. Hearing of his illness, the king visited the knight.

"What can we do for you, my friend?" asked the king. "Where is your pain?"

"Sire, the pain is in my heart," said the knight with a sigh. "I truly love your daughter, and if I cannot marry her, I shall die of sorrow."

This, of course, reminded the king of his promise to the queen. He said, "Take heart, my good fellow. You shall have your wish, for I believe that you truly love the princess."

As soon as the king had left his bedchamber, the wicked knight jumped out of bed congratulating himself on the success of his plan.

"The wedding," said the king to his ministers, "is to be the most lavish celebration this land has ever known. Let our sadness make way for great rejoicing, for my beloved queen's dearest wish is about to be granted." The king asked for the magic donkey to be brought to him. "Good beast," said the king, "you alone with your daily gifts of gold, are responsible for the luxury we enjoy. I thank you most sincerely, and hope you will continue to provide, so that this wedding will long be remembered for it's splendour."

When the princess heard that she was to marry the knight, she went to her fairy godmother for help. "Dear godmother," cried the princess, "I beg you to do something to stop this marriage."

"Calm yourself, my child," comforted the godmother. "Go to your father and tell him that you want a dress the colour of the weather, and that you will not be married until your wish is granted."

The princess did as she was told. Her father, puzzled by this strange request but wanting to please his daughter, sent for three of the finest spinners in the kingdom. "No matter what the cost," he said, "I command you to make this dress. To fail would mean severe punishment for you all."

Three days later, the spinners returned to the palace with a wonderful gown. It was delicately embroidered in subtle shades of colour which, simultaneously, seemed to reflect bright sunlight, the whiteness of soft, billowing clouds, and the grey, sombre tones of a rainy day. The princess was vexed at their success, but she thanked them graciously and hurried to her godmother.

"Very clever indeed," said the godmother scratching her head with her wand. "Well, let us see if they can spin a dress the colour of the moon. This, surely, will prove impossible."

Alas, only two days later, the talented spinners arrived with their handiwork. "Remarkable!" exclaimed the king, as the pale, translucent gown glowed like a full moon.

The godmother stamped her foot and grumbled, "Confound those spinners! In my younger days I would have turned them all into frogs. Let us try once more and ask for a dress the colour of the sun."

The king was becoming impatient at the princess's demands, but he ordered the spinners to execute this most difficult task.

Three, four, five days passed and the princess began to feel confident that her ordeal was over. But, on the sixth day, to her chagrin, the three spinners returned to show what they had accomplished. Exquisitely woven in gold thread and stitched all over with diamonds, the dress sparkled and shone exactly like the sun.

Defeated, the princess had to agree to the wedding but remained weeping in her room for three whole days. On the third day, her old godmother paid her a visit. "Be brave, dear child," she said. "I'm sure we can thwart these wedding plans. Go to the king and ask him for the skin of his magic donkey to make a coat. Everyone knows how precious this donkey is to him and he will certainly refuse."

But the godmother was wrong. Without hesitation, the king had his faithful beast slaughtered and the skin brought to his daughter. "Here is your coat!" cried the king angrily, "and since there can surely be nothing more to demand, your wedding will take place tomorrow."

The princess was in despair. During that night, while everyone slept, she pulled the donkey skin over her head, daubed soot on her

face to disguise her pale skin, and hastened from the palace. On and on she went until at last, sick with fear and exhaustion, she fell to the ground.

She was awakened by a farmer's wife saying, "You poor wretch, are you hurt?"

The princess saw above her a smiling face. "No," she whispered, "I'm just very tired and have nowhere to live."

The woman took her to the farmhouse and gave her warm milk. "If you want to stay on the farm and work," she said kindly, "I can find plenty for you to do."

By now, some of the servants had noticed the girl and were laughing at her. One said, "Look at that dirty creature wearing a donkey skin. I hope she doesn't sleep in the bed next to me."

"That's what we'll call her – Donkey-Skin!" said another, and they all burst out laughing. "Come with me," said the farmer's wife taking pity on her. "You can live in the little hut at the back of the farm."

The other servants made sure that she had all the worst jobs to do, but Donkey-Skin never complained and bore their insults silently. Each evening, weary from her work, she bolted the door of her little hut, lit her candle and took off the donkey-skin, letting her long gold tresses fall over her shoulders. Hidden under her straw mattress was a beautiful emerald ring given her by her mother before she died. Wearing this ring at night reminded the princess of happier times.

One day, the farmer's wife watched her going about her work. She saw that the girl was gentle and obedient, and very hardworking. "My child, you must be tired," she said. "Come, leave what you are doing and take the geese down to the wood." Donkey-Skin willingly obeyed her mistress and, while the geese pecked and dabbled, she sat in the warm sunshine. She was startled by the sound of a hunting horn and, not wanting to be seen by a stranger, called in the geese and drove them back to the farm.

Later, locked away in her little hut, she began to imagine who the hunter might be. "Perhaps it was the wicked knight, come to claim me for his own," she thought. Her heart fluttered as she heard the

sound of footsteps along the path. She extinguished the candle and waited.

"Is anyone there?" called a voice. Donkey-Skin remained silent.

The young man, who was a prince from a neighbouring kingdom, bent down and looked through the keyhole. His eyes rested upon the most beautiful girl he had ever seen. The rags she wore only emphasized the richness of her golden hair, her pale skin, and the glittering emerald ring on her finger. He knocked repeatedly on the door but no one answered and he walked disconsolately to the farmhouse.

"I was hunting in the forest and have lost my way," he said to the farmer's wife. She ordered a servant to bring wine and bread, and invited him to rest. The prince questioned her about the beautiful girl in the hut.

"Beautiful! Your eyes are deceiving you, sir," said the farmer's wife. "There is only our odd-job maid. Though hardworking, she is plain and always wears a coat made from the skin of a donkey."

Days passed, and the prince was unable to forget the beautiful girl. Surely she was no dream. He could find no rest and soon became ill. The queen, his mother, was so concerned that she went to her son and said, "What ails you, my dear son? What can we do to restore you to good health?" The prince scarce knew what he was saying, but he asked for a cake baked by the beautiful girl who lives in a little hut near the forest.

A messenger was sent in great haste to seek out this mysterious girl. When at last he reached the little hut, Donkey-Skin, opened the door to him. The queen's messenger was startled at the sight of a dirty maid dressed in a donkey skin, but he obeyed his instructions and explained why she must bake a cake. Donkey-Skin felt compassion for the prince and agreed to have the cake ready for the messenger to collect the following day.

That night, when she had removed the donkey skin, washed her golden locks and put on her emerald ring, she began to mix the cake. As she stirred, the ring fell unnoticed into the bowl. The cake was collected the next morning and taken to the palace. When the prince cut into it, he discovered the ring. His heart leapt, for as he recognised the emerald he knew it had not been a dream. "Bring me the owner of this ring," he commanded, "and, whoever she is, I shall make her my bride!"

When the royal messenger returned with Donkey-Skin, everyone gasped, for she looked so poor and neglected. But she held out her hand for the ring. It slipped easily on to her middle finger.

The prince was quickly restored to health and Donkey-Skin was reunited with her father, who gladly consented to the marriage. At the ceremony, when the beautiful bride walked in, looking every inch a royal princess in her wonderful dress the colour of the sun, the happy king turned to the fairy godmother and said:

"I am content. This young prince did, most truly, almost die for love of her!"

Hans Christian Andersen 1805–1875

Born in Odense, Denmark, Hans Christian Andersen was the son of a poor shoemaker. By nature a romantic dreamer, young Hans' earliest ambitions were theatrical. He tried singing, dancing, acting and reciting before eventually achieving success as a playwright, novelist and writer of children's fairy stories. His early struggle to discover where his true talents lay, emphasized by his lack of early education and physical unattractiveness, is reflected in his most famous story – The Ugly Duckling.

The Ugly Duckling

It was summertime; the corn was golden, the oats were green, the hay was stacked in the meadows, and the long red-legged stork strutted about.

Beyond the meadows on the edge of a forest, stood an old manor-house. It was surrounded by a deep moat and, from its crumbling walls down to the water's edge grew large burdock leaves. Here, sheltered and quiet in this wild and beautiful spot, a duck had chosen to build her nest. She sat on her eggs, waiting for them to hatch so that she could join her friends for a gossip along the canal bank.

Before long, the eggs cracked open one after the other. "Peep! Peep!" the little ducklings said, sticking their heads out of the shells. They waddled about, peering around in wonder, under the green burdock leaves. Their mother got up from her nest, thinking that all the eggs had been hatched. Then she noticed that there was still one egg left, a very large one, so she settled down again.

At last, the big egg broke. "Peep! Peep!" cried the new arrival as he tumbled out. Mother duck looked horrified! He was big, grey, and ugly. "Could it be a turkey-chick and not a duckling?" she wondered. "We'll soon see. First thing in the morning, into the water he'll go, even if I have to push him in myself!"

Next day, the sun shone down on the burdock leaves. Mother duck took all her little ones down to the canal. Splash! – she plunged into the water. "Come along, all of you," she called, as one duckling after another tumbled in. The water closed over their heads, but they all bobbed straight up again and swam about effortlessly, even the ugly grey duckling.

"That's no turkey!" thought mother duck with a sigh of relief. "See how well he uses his legs, and how erect he holds his head. My baby," she whispered tenderly, and proudly led her brood along to the farmyard to meet some friends.

The noise was deafening. Two duck families were fighting over a fish-head. Suddenly a large black cat crept into the yard and pounced on the fish-head before any of the ducks knew what was happening. "That's the way of the world," warned mother duck. "Always be on the alert for cats! Now, show your good manners, and go and bow your heads to that old duck over there. She is of royal blood – and commands the greatest respect. Hurry now, and don't turn in your toes! Bow nicely and say quack, quack!"

The other ducks glared peevishly at them. "Not another bunch of ducklings!" they complained. "Don't you think there are enough of us here already? And as for that ugly grey monster, we don't want him staying in the farmyard." And one duck flew straight at him and pecked him on the neck.

"Leave him alone, you big bully," cried mother duck.

The stately old duck intervened. "Stop this at once!" she scolded, and waddled her way around the new family. "They are a credit to you," she nodded approvingly to mother duck. "But whatever went wrong with this one?" – and all eyes turned on the ugly duckling.

"Oh, I know he's not handsome, your ladyship," said mother duck apologetically, "but surely that matters little in a drake. He is very kind and is the strongest of them all," she added. She stroked the back of his neck fondly and smoothed his feathers.

And so the new family settled in with the other ducks. That is, all but the ugly duckling, who was teased and pecked and pushed around by hens and ducks and turkeys alike. He soon became the laughing stock of the farmyard.

Things grew worse as the days went by; even his own brothers and sisters turned their backs on him saying: "I wish the cat would carry you off, you ugly creature!"

At last, his poor mother, tired of seeing him cry, sighed, "For your own good, I wish you were far away from here!"

That night, the little duckling fluttered over the hedge and ran as fast and as far as his legs would carry him until, exhausted, he settled down in a clump of reeds on a great marsh where the wild ducks lived.

At sunrise, when the wild ducks spotted the newcomer, they remarked, "Whatever kind of duck are you? You are quite remarkably ugly!" Poor duckling! All he wanted was to be allowed to rest among the reeds, and drink a little water. He lay there for two whole days feeling quite wretched, wondering what to do and where to go.

Then two young high-flying ganders arrived on the scene. "Hey there, ugly face!" they called, "Keep away from the lake! Some handsome geese have just settled there and we're going to pay them court. If they see you, they'll fly away in terror!"

And off they went, their jeers and laughter echoing on the wind. Almost at once, there was a loud bang-bang! The ugly duckling looked up and saw the two ganders who had mocked him plumetting into the marsh! The hunters had arrived!

Dogs splashed through the water, barking and baying. The terrified duckling tucked his head under his wing, his little heart pounding fit to burst. An enormous dog bounded towards him. "Help me, dear mother!" whispered the duckling. The dog snarled at the still, feathery creature at his feet. Then at the sound of a whistle, turned and bounded off in the opposite direction. "I must be too ugly even for the dog!" thought the duckling. The commotion lasted for several hours, with the sound of guns and the occasional cry of some unfortunate creature. When all was silent again, the duckling fled from the marsh as fast as he could.

Autumn came, the leaves turned yellow, then brown, and a chill

wind nipped the air. One evening, at sunset, a flock of large, handsome birds appeared across the lake. The duckling had never seen anything quite so beautiful. They were dazzling white, with long slender necks and magnificent wings. The little duckling felt a strange thrill as he watched them rise higher into the sky. He turned round and round in the water like a wheel, and craned his neck towards them, letting out a cry so shrill that he startled himself. "Oh, what beautiful, lucky birds," he thought; and as soon as they were out of sight he dived right down to the bottom with excitement.

When he bobbed up again, he was almost beside himself. He did not know what they were called, or where they were flying to, but he loved them more than he had ever loved anyone before. He wished he could be like them.

The winter was cruel. The duckling was forced to swim about in the water to prevent it from freezing under him. But every night, the hole in which he swam became smaller and smaller. It froze so hard that the duckling had to keep his legs moving all the time to stop the ice from closing in. At last, exhausted, he froze fast into the ice.

Early in the morning, a farmer was passing by. Seeing the duckling, he went down to him, broke the ice with his clog and carried him home to his wife. There the duckling revived.

The children wanted to play with him, but he was afraid of them and flew in panic into the milk pan, so that milk splashed all over the room. The farmer's wife shouted and clapped her hands, which frightened the duckling even more. He flew into the butter-tub and from there into the flour bin and out again. What a sight he looked! The woman screamed, and struck at him with the broom while the children tumbled over one another trying to catch him. Luckily, the door stood open, and the poor creature was able to dart out into the bushes and hide himself in the soft snow.

It would be too sad a story to tell you of all the misery and suffering the duckling had to endure that bitterly cold winter. But one day, he was sheltering among the rushes by the lake when the sun shone warmly again. The larks began to sing. Spring had returned!

He tried his wings. They were stronger than before and carried him higher into the clear air. Before he realised it, he found himself over a large garden, where apple-trees blossomed and fragrant lilacs hung their long green branches over a stream. How soft and fresh it all was. Then, floating lightly over the water, came three beautiful white swans. The duckling recognized the magnificent birds and was overcome with a strange sadness.

"I will go to them," he thought. I know they will kill me because I am so ugly, but I'd rather be pecked to death by them than be ill used by hens, and ducks, and all the other farmyard animals, and then to suffer another lonely winter!" He swam towards the swans. They ruffled their feathers and preened themselves. "Kill me!" cried the duckling, and bowed his head, awaiting death.

But what did he see reflected in the clear stream? Looking back at him from the water was – not a grey, ugly duckling – but a graceful, long-necked swan! The big swans swam round him, and stroked him with their beaks.

"Look! There's a new swan!" cried some children running along the bank. They threw corn and bread to him in the water. "Isn't he

the most beautiful of them all?" And the older swans bowed their heads to him.

For a moment or two, he felt quite shy and hid his head under his wings. He thought of how he had been persecuted and despised; and now everyone was saying that he was the most beautiful swan of them all. Overcome with joy, he ruffled his feathers, lifted his long slender neck, and from his heart cried: "I never dreamed of so much happiness when I was the ugly duckling!"

The Snail and the Briar

The garden was surrounded by a hazel hedge, beyond which lay green meadows where cows and sheep grazed peacefully. In the middle of the garden a rose-tree bloomed, and beneath its fragrant branches sat a snail.

The snail spent his time just being himself. "You wait!" he said smugly. "My time will come, and when it does I shall do much more than carry scented blossoms, or yield hazel nuts, or even provide milk like those simple cows and sheep."

"I am expecting such great things of you," said the rose-tree. "May I be permitted to enquire when your time is to be?"

"Why are you in such a hurry?" asked the snail. "Be patient."

A year later, the snail had hardly moved from his spot under the rose-tree, where buds were just beginning to open into roses, always fresh and new. He raised his feelers slowly, and said, "Everything looks exactly the same as a year ago. The roses are the same shape and

colour as last year. There are no exciting developments with the hazel hedge. In fact, it seems to me that for all their activity they are extremely limited!"

Summer passed, the Autumn rushed by, and still the roses bloomed in all their glory, until the weather turned cold and damp, and snow began to fall. Then the rose-tree stooped towards the ground and the snail crawled into the earth.

The garden looked desolate as it slept under a thick blanket of snow, but as the icy blasts gave way to fresh winds which quickly blew away the last traces of a long winter, everything began to come alive again, and the snail appeared in his usual spot under the rose-tree.

"You're turning into an old broom," he sneered, "and soon there will be nothing left of you but thorns. After so much effort, you still have nothing more important to offer the world than your pretty scented roses. Has it really been worth it?"

"You frighten me with your clever words!" said the rose-tree, "but all I can say is that I blossom with joy, – I just cannot help myself. I feel the warm sunshine, breathe the fresh air, and drink the clear dew and rain. Strength seeps into me from the soil. I live and blossom with happiness. That is the reason for my life!"

"Huh!" said the snail. "You lead a very pleasant life!"

"Yes, indeed. I have everything!" agreed the rose-tree. "Yet you have been blessed with much greater gifts. You are of a thinking, enquiring nature. You have great talents which will astound the world."

"The world!" said the snail. "I don't care about the world!"

"But shouldn't we all give what we are capable of?" said the rose-tree. "I know, of course, that I only give roses – but what about you? With all of your intelligence, what have you given of yourself?"

"What have I given? What am I giving the world? I spit on the world! It is worthless and to me uninteresting. Give it your flowers. After all, that's the only thing you are capable of! Let the hazel bush give its nuts, and the cows and sheep their milk – somebody will have use for them. But I have use only for myself! I shall crawl into my shell, and there I'll remain." With that, the snail crawled into his house and sealed it up.

"How sad!" said the rose-tree. "With the best will in the world I can't crawl away like that; I have to keep on budding and growing roses, even though their petals fall and the wind blows them away. Yet I have seen a woman place one of my roses in her hymn-book, and another rose of mine was held tenderly and kissed by a child. These things I shall never forget. They give meaning to my life." And

the rose-tree, in its innocence, blossomed on, while the snail lazed about in his shell, not caring about anything.

And so the years passed. The earth buried the snail. The earth buried the rose-tree; the rose in the hymn-book turned to dust, but in the garden new rose-trees bloomed and made the world a better place. Also in the garden new snails grew; they crawled into their little shells, caring not in the least about the world.

If we were to start at the beginning again – the tale would be exactly the same.

The Nightingale

Long ago, in China, there lived a mighty Emperor. His palace was said to be the most magnificent in the whole world. It was made entirely of the finest porcelain; so fragile and delicate that one hardly dared touch it.

The palace gardens were exquisite and so vast that not even the gardeners who tended them knew exactly where they ended. Flowers bloomed everywhere, and to the most splendid of these were fastened little silver bells, which tinkled so that no one would pass by without admiring them.

Beyond the gardens lay a forest with tall trees which stretched right down to the blue sea. In the branches of one of the trees at the water's edge lived a nightingale. Each night she would sing so sweetly that even the poor fishermen, who were busily casting their nets, would stop and listen.

Travellers came from all over the world to see and to write about the Emperor's city. They marvelled at the splendour but once hearing the little nightingale, they all agreed that no treasure could compare with the simple beauty of her song.

One day a book was brought to the throne room. It had been sent as a gift from the Emperor of Japan. His Imperial Majesty sat happily turning the pages and nodding his approval at the wonderful descriptions of his city, but when he read, "The best of all these treasures is the nightingale," he called at once for his gentleman-in-waiting.

"I have read in this book," began the Emperor loudly, "that a remarkable bird called a nightingale lives in the forest beyond my garden. Her song, it is said, is more beautiful than anything else in the whole of my empire! Why have I never been told of this?"

"Your Imperial Majesty," said the gentleman-in-waiting, "I have never heard of this nightingale."

"Then go at once and find her!" commanded the Emperor. "I wish her to come and sing for me."

The gentleman-in-waiting was a proud man and not used to speaking to anyone of inferior rank. How was he to find this nightingale? He would have to bring himself to enquire amongst the servants. The very idea brought a blush to his cheeks. He ran up one flight of steps, down another, through the halls and corridors, questioning everyone. But no one had ever heard of this wondrous nightingale. In desperation, the gentleman-in-waiting returned to the Emperor and, bowing low, declared, "Your Imperial Majesty would be wise not to believe everything that is written in books. Much of it is pure fiction."

The Emperor's mouth tightened with anger. "But this book was sent to me by the powerful Emperor of Japan. It must be true!" Before the gentleman-in-waiting could muster up enough courage to disagree, the Emperor continued, "The nightingale must be found and brought to me this evening. If she does not come, I will have the whole Court flogged after supper!"

In a panic, the gentleman-in-waiting rushed up and down the stairs again and through the halls and corridors with half the Royal Court behind him, for no one relished the idea of being flogged. At last, the gentleman-in-waiting visited the royal kitchens where only the most humble of the Emperor's servants worked.

He questioned the chief washer-up, who called to his side a poor little kitchen-maid. "Yes, my lord," she said shyly, "I've heard the nightingale! Each evening I am allowed to take a few scraps from the table to my sick mother who lives in a hut down by the sea-shore. On my way back, when I feel tired and stop to rest, I hear the nightingale sing. Her song is as sweet as my dear mother's kiss."

The gentleman-in-waiting gave a great sigh of relief. "Dear little kitchen-maid," he said, "lead us to where we may find this wonderful bird and you shall be immediately promoted to a better position in the Emperor's kitchen, even with permission to watch His Majesty eat!"

So the little kitchen-maid led the gentleman-in-waiting, and a great number of the courtiers, into the woods. As they crossed the meadow, a cow began to bellow. "Listen!" whispered a courtier. "There it is! What a lovely sound."

"Oh no," said the little kitchen-maid. "That is only a cow lowing."

Presently, some frogs began croaking in a nearby pond. "I hear her now!" cried the Court Chaplain. "It's like the sound of church bells."

"Those are frogs croaking," said the kitchen-maid. "But now we are getting very near."

Then the nightingale began to sing. "Listen! Listen! There she sits," and the kitchen-maid pointed to a grey bird up in the branches of a tree.

"What a common little bird!" exclaimed the gentleman-in-waiting.

"Little nightingale!" cried the kitchen-maid, "our noble Emperor wishes you to sing for him this evening. Will you come?"

"With great pleasure," said the nightingale, "although my song sounds far better in the woods."

So the little nightingale followed the procession back to the palace and sang so charmingly that she touched the hearts of all who heard her. The Emperor ordered that a festival should be held in honour of the nightingale. A golden perch was erected in the grand hall, near to the throne. The porcelain palace glittered in the light of a thousand gold lamps, and the loveliest flowers, with the merriest tinkling bells, were placed everywhere.

As darkness fell, all the courtiers took their places in the grand hall. The little kitchen-maid had received permission to stand behind the door, for she had now been given the rank and title of "Maid of the Kitchen." There was a pause as His Imperial Majesty entered and seated himself on his golden throne. Everybody waited in silence until the little nightingale flew through the window and began to sing.

Words cannot describe the pure sweetness of the grey bird's song.

Tears came into the Emperor's eyes and rolled down his cheeks. Restless page boys sat motionless and the ladies-in-waiting were quite overcome by the joyful sound. "The nightingale shall have my golden slippers and wear them round her neck!" announced the delighted Emperor.

But the nightingale replied in her softest tones, "The tears of joy in Your Imperial Majesty's eyes are reward enough."

Presently there was a royal announcement that the little bird was to remain at court and have her very own golden cage. Permission would be granted for her to fly to the forest twice a day. On these occasions she would be accompanied by twelve attendants, each holding tightly to a silken ribbon fastened to the bird's feet, to ensure that she returned to the palace to sing to the Emperor each night.

The nightingale soon became famous. At street corners, poets read aloud their verses paying tribute to her lovely songs. His Imperial Majesty came to depend on her nightly visits. Never had he felt so happy.

One day, a parcel arrived at the palace. "Yet another book about our song-bird!" said the Emperor. But instead, it was a box containing a clockwork nightingale, covered with diamonds, rubies and sapphires. When wound up it sang one of the songs which the real nightingale sang, to absolute perfection. In the box was a message saying,

> *The nightingale of the Emperor of China is a poor drab creature compared with the nightingale of the Emperor of Japan.*

The Emperor was very annoyed when he read these words and cried, "We shall see!" Then he summoned the Royal Watchmaker. "Let them sing together," he commanded. "Surely this artificial bird cannot match the sweetness of my real nightingale."

And so the duet began. The clockwork toy's song was perfect and quite as pure as the nightingale's. Again and again, the clockwork bird was wound up and, each time, it sang as prettily and as tunefully as the last. The real nightingale began to grow weary for she had never sung the same song twice. After a while, seeing that everyone's eyes were focused on the brilliant toy, she escaped through an open window and flew towards her own green forest.

"What is the meaning of this?" cried the Emperor when he realised that his real song-bird was no longer there.

"Such an ungrateful bird!" commented the courtiers. "But we still have the best of the pair!"

His Imperial Majesty was so enchanted with his new toy that he ordered another court festival to which he invited all the people from the city. "Magnificent!" they all said, after hearing the clockwork toy. "Such brilliance! Surely our Emperor has the most precious object in the world."

Only the poor fishermen, who were used to hearing the real nightingale, said, "It's a pretty sound, but there is no variety."

Time passed, and the Emperor, the Court, and all of the Chinese people knew every clink and cluck of the mechanical bird's song. Then a terrible thing happened. Just as the watchmaker wound up the toy for the Emperor's evening entertainment, there was a sudden snap, followed by an ugly whirring sound and then silence! "Do something!" cried the Emperor, "or I will have you flogged!"

The watchmaker carried the glittering, tuneless toy to his workshop and, with great skill, took apart all the delicate pieces, cleaned them, and replaced them. Pale-faced, he returned to the throne room and said, "Your Imperial Majesty, I have repaired the bird, but as many of the parts are almost worn out, I beg of you, do not have me wind it up more than once a year." This was a mighty blow to the Emperor, who had come to love the nightingale's song more than anything else.

Five years passed and the Emperor became very ill. It was the considered opinion of the Royal Physician that His Imperial Majesty could not survive more than a few days. As he lay in his magnificent bed with it's long velvet curtains and heavy gold tassels, the Emperor gazed sadly at the silent clockwork toy. "How foolish I have been," he whispered, "to place this glittering object above that little grey bird from the woods. If only I could hear her lovely song once more."

The Emperor was fading fast. In his imaginings, a ghostly spectre sat at the foot of his bed wearing the Royal Crown and holding the Imperial Banner. Other phantoms appeared in the dim light of his bed-chamber. Some with a gentle look, and others with an expression so hideous that his failing heart froze with fear. They were the good and bad deeds of the Emperor's life, come to take their reckoning. Sweat broke out upon his forehead and his eyelids drooped.

All at once in the darkness, the sweetest sound was heard from outside the window. It was the little nightingale! She sang of hope and joy and all the beautiful things in nature; of trees and flowers and the sweet, fresh smell of the blessed earth. As she sang, the ghostly figures became paler and vanished from the bedchamber, and the Emperor fell into a deep, peaceful sleep.

The next morning, the Emperor awoke feeling strong and healthy. None of his servants had returned during the night for they all believed him to be dead. When the gentleman-in-waiting finally ventured into the royal bedchamber, he was amazed to see His Imperial Majesty sitting up in bed!

"No, I am not a ghost!" said the Emperor. "I have been restored to life by my own little grey nightingale."

And from that day on, the little nightingale visited the Emperor each evening. Never again was she confined to a cage, but was allowed complete freedom to come and go as she wished.

Jean de la Fontaine 1621–1695

Elder son of the superintendent of waters and forests of Château-Thierry in Champagne, La Fontaine became a renowned poet and was the author of the Fables – a collection of some two hundred and forty poems, published in various editions between 1668 and 1694. The material for the Fables is largely drawn from Aesop, but also from other classical, Eastern and modern sources.

The Hare and the Tortoise

One fresh spring morning as the sun rose, a young hare preened himself and, feeling in a boastful mood, looked around for someone to impress.

His friends were not yet about and there were only a few birds testing their wings. "I challenge any of you to a race," called the hare to a couple of passing magpies.

"Don't be silly," cried one of the magpies. "We're far too busy feathering our nests just now. Another time perhaps." And off they flew.

"I'll take up your challenge," called a sleepy voice, as a tortoise peered out from a clump of buttercups and lumbered towards the hare.

"Run a race with you, old lazybones?" scoffed the hare indignantly. "What a joke! I could run rings round you all the way."

"Then you are quite at liberty to do so, my swift-footed friend," said the tortoise. "But if I were you, I would save my boasting until I had won the race. Shall we begin?"

The hare couldn't resist an opportunity to show off his talents and so, in the presence of a large crow, who agreed to act as umpire, they set the course for the race. The crow gave instructions for the contestants to line up and, with a loud 'C A W', the race began.

At once, the hare ran at full speed and was soon out of sight. He was so sure of winning, that he decided to take a nap on a mossy cushion before starting his return journey. Within seconds, he was asleep. Meanwhile, the tortoise plodded on, across the meadow, through the wood and back until he was within sight of the winning post.

The hare awoke with a start and, not realising how long he had slept, ran swiftly back through the wood feeling well-rested and confident.

When he reached the meadow, he heard loud cheering and saw a crow waiting by the winning post. "It can't be. No, it's not possible!" he said to himself, making a last dash across the meadow.

But he was too late. There in front of him, just crossing over the winning line was Old Lazybones.

The Fox and the Stork

A crafty young fox invited a stork to dinner one day. Thinking that he would provide himself with an afternoon's entertainment at his guest's expense, he offered some clear soup in a wide, shallow dish. The fox, trying to keep a straight face, lapped his soup with gusto, while watching the stork assume the most amazing positions in an attempt to draw the soup up the length of her long, slender beak. Alas, it was impossible.

"Forgive me," said the fox, "the soup is obviously not to your liking! Permit me to relieve you of it." And the cunning rascal quickly drank his guest's portion.

The stork felt most offended at having been made to look ridiculous but, determined to get her own back on the fox, she smiled graciously and said, "It would give me such pleasure to return your

hospitality. Will you be my guest tomorrow evening?"

"Delighted," replied the fox, and added, "Not a scrap shall pass my lips all day, so that I can do justice to your excellent cooking."

At exactly the appointed time, the fox presented himself at the stork's abode. A most delicious smell was coming from the kitchen. "Ah! Beef stew!" sighed the fox, who was by now quite ravenous.

"Come, my friend," said the hostess with a smile, "take a seat at the table and allow me to serve you." The fox gladly obeyed and sat, eyes closed, rapturously sniffing the wonderful aroma. "Do start!" announced the stork, placing two steaming, tall flagons on the table. The fox stared in dismay.

"Mmmm . . . this new recipe is a great success," said the stork, using her long beak to reach to the bottom of the vessel.

The fox stood on his chair and pushed his nose into the neck of the flagon until it hurt. "I can't reach it," he cried impatiently.

"What a pity!" said the stork. "Then I suppose I shall have to eat it myself. Kindly pass it across the table, will you?"

The fox looked furious. "Madam," he said, "I think you are most unkind to treat me in this way. If this is your idea of hospitality, I shall leave at once."

"As you wish," answered the stork politely. "You set the example yourself, so you should really not complain when I follow it."

The Country Mouse and the Town Mouse

A simple country mouse received a visit one day from an old friend who lived in the town. It had been a long time since the two shared happy hours together in the fields as youngsters, and, when Town Mouse arrived looking every inch the sophisticated mouse-about-town, Country Mouse could hardly recognise his old playmate.

After a warm welcome and a few polite exchanges, Country Mouse offered his friend the most comfortable of his rickety chairs while he busied himself preparing a meal. It was not a rich feast, but it was the very best Country Mouse could offer from his frugal pantry. There was a bowl of delicate grey peas flavoured with a few scraps of bacon, some cheese, and a remnant of mellow apple served as dessert. Good manners prevented Country Mouse from sharing the meal in case his visitor should not have enough to eat, but, in the tradition of all good hosts, he entertained his guest with polite conversation whilst nibbling on a piece of straw.

Town Mouse, however, was not used to such simple fare and only picked at the food. At last he pushed away his plate and with a look of some disdain said, "Old fellow, forgive my bluntness, but how on earth can you live in this melancholy hole, with nothing but meadows and woods all around you and a few peas and scraps of bacon to eat?"

Country Mouse listened in embarrassed silence as his friend went on. "Come with me to the town where the streets are busy and the air is full of excitement. Don't you long to live in luxury and dine on fine foods?" Country Mouse could only nod.

“Life is short, my friend,” continued Town Mouse, “and we must enjoy every moment to the full, for who knows what might happen tomorrow.” Much as he tried, Country Mouse could not argue with this statement and he agreed to accompany his friend to town that very night.

The noisy streets and bright lights of the town terrified the country dweller, but, determined not to show fear, he doggedly followed Town Mouse to his home. It was richer and grander than anything Country Mouse had imagined. There were soft velvet couches, precious ornaments, and beautiful warm carpets, and on the magnificent dining table stood the remains of a splendid banquet.

Now it was the turn of Town Mouse to act as host. He presented his humble guest with dish after dish of the most delicious food, tasting everything himself first to make sure that it had been properly cooked. Red wine was served with a dish of red jelly and an excellent white wine was offered with the cream.

Country Mouse enjoyed every mouthful, but just as he was about to sink back into the lush carpet for an after dinner snooze, he heard the loud barking of dogs. Panic stricken, he sat huddled in a corner whilst two large mastiffs burst into the room and went sniffing about in every nook and cranny.

"This way!" cried Town Mouse, as he squeezed through a crack under the window seat.

Safe outside, Town Mouse patted his trembling friend on the back and said, "Nothing like a bit of excitement, old fellow. When the noise dies down, we'll go back inside."

"Not I," said Country Mouse. "If this is the life you lead, you are welcome to it. Give me my simple, quiet, uneventful hole again. Goodbye, my friend. Come and visit me when you need a rest." And off he went, to his peaceful meadows, his woods, and his homely grey peas.

Jacob Ludwig Karl Grimm 1785–1863

Wilhelm Karl Grimm 1786–1859

Known universally, The Brothers Grimm were born in Hanau, near Frankfurt, Germany, sons of a lawyer. Their famous tales were the result of many years research into the traditional folk-lore and legendary tales of Germany handed down by word of mouth throughout successive generations. A collection of the stories, originally known as *Kinder-und-Hausmärchen (Nursery and Household Tales)* were translated into many languages and won world-wide fame.

The Musicians of Bremen Town

There was once a donkey who had been a faithful servant to his master for a great many years. As he grew old, however, and slow to do his work, his master began to think of putting an end to him; but the donkey sensed that something dreadful was about to happen and, before his master awoke one morning, ran out of his field and off down the road towards Bremen town. "There," he thought, "I'll be able to use all my talents and become a musician!"

Further along the road he met a dog, panting as if he were about to die. "What's the matter friend?" asked the donkey.

"I'm running away!" gasped the dog. "My master says that I'm too fat and old to run with the hounds anymore. He beat me yesterday for falling asleep over my bowl of food. I can't bear the disgrace any-more!"

"Look here, old friend," said Donkey kindly, "why don't you come with me. I'm going to Bremen town to become a musician."

"Oh, could I?" said Dog, at once feeling a good deal better. "My bark is well known in these parts for its richness of tone." So the two friends jogged along together.

Presently, they came across a bedraggled little cat sitting in the middle of the road with her eyes half shut.

"Excuse me, ma'am," said Donkey politely. "Is there anything we can do to help?"

The cat gave a sad meow and tried to clean her soaking wet fur. "I've just escaped from being drowned by my mistress," she wailed, "at whose feet I've laid more than a thousand mice!"

"I suppose the mice have got too clever for you," said Dog, giving her head a gentle lick.

"Yes," nodded the cat sadly. "I'm too old to chase them and prefer to lie by the fireside." She began to cry.

Donkey cleared his throat and said, "Why don't you come with us to Bremen town? A good night singer like you could make a fortune as a musician."

"Oh thank you, dear friends," she purred, and gave her tail a cheerful flick.

Soon afterwards, they met a handsome rooster perched on a farmyard gate. "What a to-do! What a to-do!" he crowed.

"You sound very upset over something," said Donkey. "What's the matter?"

"I've just learned that some guests are coming on Sunday, and I am to be their dinner! What a to-do!" crowed the rooster. "Whatever shall I do!"

"Heaven forbid!" said Donkey. "You must come with us. We need a powerful voice like yours to reach the top notes." After Donkey and his friends had explained where they were going, and for what reason, the rooster flew on to Donkey's back and the four of them set off together.

By nightfall, they had reached the edge of a dense forest and decided to rest there until daybreak. "I'll stand guard," said Rooster,

and found a perfect lookout position at the top of a tall tree. The others made themselves comfortable on a bed of dry leaves. Rooster looked all around and saw in the distance something bright and shining. "There must be a house over there!" he called down to his companions.

Donkey shook his ears and yawned. "Perhaps we'd better take a look," he said.

"There may be some food lying around," said Dog, who was feeling very hungry.

At the mention of food, Cat stretched herself. "Do let's go," she purred. "There may even be a warm fire to curl up by."

Now the house was a hideout for a gang of robbers. As the four friends approached under cover of darkness, they could hear voices coming from the house. "Cat!" whispered Donkey urgently. "Can you climb up and look through the window?" Silently she leapt onto the window ledge and looked in. "Well, what do you see?" asked Donkey.

Cat hissed nervously. "There are some rough looking men sitting round a table laden with bottles and food. I can see knives and guns. One of the men is slumped over the table. I think they are all drowsy from the wine they have drunk." Cat hissed again and jumped down to join her friends.

"We'll have to have a meeting about this!" announced Donkey gravely. They put their heads together and whispered feverishly.

"That's the plan then!" growled Dog, his hackles rising.

They waited in the shadows until all that could be heard from the house was the noise of loud snores. "Now!" said Donkey, standing by the window. Dog immediately jumped on to Donkey's back. Cat scrambled on to Dog's shoulders and Rooster flew up and perched himself on the top of Cat's head.

"Start the music!" cried Donkey with a deafening bray. Dog howled, Cat meowed, and Rooster crowed like he'd never done

before. At the same moment Donkey smashed the window with his front hooves and the animals stormed into the room, biting, scratching, pecking and kicking.

The terrified robbers, certain that they were being attacked by some monstrous demons, took to their heels and disappeared into the forest.

"What a magnificent performance!" said Donkey proudly, and they all sat down to enjoy the food the robbers had left behind.

As soon as they had satisfied themselves, they each sought out a resting place. Donkey laid himself upon a heap of straw in the yard. Dog stretched out on a mat behind the door. Cat rolled herself up on the hearth before the warm embers, and Rooster perched on a beam.

At about midnight, when the robbers saw from afar that the lights were out, they began to think that they had perhaps been in too great a hurry to run away. One of them, bolder than the rest, went to see what was going on. Finding everything quiet, he crept into the kitchen and groped around for a match. Then, noticing the fiery eyes of Cat, he mistook them for live coals and held the match to them to light it. Cat sprung at his face and scratched him. Shocked and frightened, the man ran to the back door, but there Dog jumped up and bit him on the leg. As he ran across the yard, Donkey kicked him and Rooster, who had been awakened by the noise, crowed with all his might. The robber ran back to his comrades as fast as he could.

"A witch has got into the house," he cried. "She scratched my face with her long bony fingers. Then a man came at me from behind the door and stabbed me in the leg. When I ran out into the yard, a monster struck me with a club, and terrifying screeches were coming from the top of the house."

After hearing this, the robbers never dared return to the house, but the musicians, well pleased with their new abode, settled down to a new and happy life together.

The Frog Prince

One fine summer evening, a young princess went walking in the woods. She took with her a tiny golden ball which was her favourite toy. After a while, she sat down by a cool stream and amused herself by throwing her ball into the air and catching it as it fell. Higher and higher she threw the ball, until at last she missed her catch and the ball splashed into the stream. The water was very deep at that point with rocks covering the bottom. It was impossible to see where the ball had fallen. She began to cry and said, "I would gladly give away all of my fine clothes and jewels if only I could have my golden ball again."

While she was speaking, a frog popped its head out of the water, and said, "Princess, do not weep so bitterly, I will help you."

"Alas!" cried the princess, "what can an ugly little frog like you do to help me? My beautiful toy is lost for ever in the depths of the stream."

"I have no use for your jewels or fine clothes," said the frog, "but I will find your ball for you on one condition."

"What is that?" asked the princess eagerly.

"You must make me a promise that I may eat with you from a golden plate and sleep upon your bed!" The princess was amazed at this strange request, but would have agreed to anything in order to get back her golden ball.

So the frog dived deep under the water, and moments later reappeared with the precious toy in his mouth. The princess was so overjoyed that she snatched the ball and ran back to the palace.

In vain the little frog called, "Wait princess! Do not forget your

promise!" But she was already out of sight.

That evening, as the princess sat in her bedchamber, she heard a tap-tapping noise on the door, and then a tiny voice calling,

Open the door, my princess dear,
Open the door to your true love here!
And mind the promise that you made
By the cool stream in the greenwood shade.

The princess opened the door, and there sat the frog, whom she had quite forgotten. She was startled and ran past the frog and down the marble staircase calling to her parents.

"There is a horrid frog at the door of my bedchamber," she cried. "It was he who gave me back my golden ball when I had lost it in the stream this morning. I promised that if he retrieved the ball, he could eat with me at the palace and sleep upon my bed; and now he is at my door wanting to come in!"

The king spoke kindly but firmly to his daughter, and said, "As you have made a solemn promise to this frog, so you must keep it. Now go and let him in, but do not fear, a frog cannot harm you."

Somewhat ashamed of herself, the princess returned to her bedchamber to find the frog still sitting outside the door. "Come in," she said, "and I will send for food that you may eat."

The frog ate heartily from a golden plate and then said, "I am tired. Lift me on to your pillow that I may sleep." The princess gently placed the frog upon her pillow where he slept all night long.

At daybreak, he jumped up, hopped down the marble staircase and left the palace. "Good riddance!" thought the princess. "I shall be troubled with the horrid frog no more." But she was mistaken; for that evening, in her bedchamber, she heard the same tap-tapping on the door. When she opened it, the frog hopped in, ate his supper and slept another night upon her pillow, leaving at daybreak as before.

On the third night, the same thing happened; but when the princess awoke the next morning, she was astonished to find, not a frog, but the most handsome prince she had ever seen, standing at her bedside.

The prince told her that he had been cursed by a wicked fairy, who had changed him into a frog. The spell could only be broken when a princess offered him food from a golden plate, and allowed him to sleep upon her bed for three nights. "You, sweet princess," said the prince, "have lifted this cruel curse, and now my dearest wish is that you should accompany me to my father's kingdom as my bride."

The princess happily consented to marry the handsome prince, and they were soon carried off to the prince's palace in a splendid coach drawn by eight beautiful horses, where they lived happily for a great many years.

The Tom-Tit and the Bear

One fine day, as the wolf and the bear were walking together in a wood, they heard a bird singing most charmingly. "Dear friend," said the bear, "what is the name of that delightful bird?"

"Ah!" said the wolf, "that is his highness the king of the air. We must take care to show him every respect." (Now I should tell you that this bird was, after all, none other than the tom-tit.)

"If that is the case," said the bear, "I should very much like to see his royal palace; so pray show it to me."

"Not so fast, comrade," said the wolf, "we must be patient and wait."

Soon afterwards, the queen appeared with food in her beak, and she and the king began to feed their young ones.

"Now, let's see!" said the bear.

"Stop!" cried the wolf. "We must not go near until their majesties are gone again." So they carefully marked the hole where the birds were nesting and crept quietly away. The bear, however, being eager to see the royal palace, soon returned and, peeping into the nest, saw five young birds lying snugly at the bottom of it.

"Is this all there is to see? What nonsense!" growled the bear. "This is no royal palace, and you," he glared indignantly at the little birds, "are nothing but base-born brats!"

As soon as the young tom-tits heard this, they screamed back angrily,"We are not base-born, you stupid bear! Our father and mother are good honest folk. You shall suffer for your insolence!"

At this the bear was frightened, and ran to tell his friend the wolf what had happened. The young tom-tits however, carried on screaming until their father and mother returned with more food. Together, they all cried, "We will not touch a morsel, no, not even the leg of a fly, though we should die of starvation, until that disrespectful bruin has been punished for his insults."

"Rest assured, my darlings," said the king indulgently, "he shall be made to eat his words."

So the king scratched out a declaration on a piece of bark. It read:

To Bruin the Bear:

We, the undersigned, do hereby declare bloody and cruel war upon you and your kind, which shall continue until suitable punishment has been administered to the richly deserving offender.

signed . . . **The Royal Society of Feathers**

Now when the bear read this, he called a meeting between the ox, the ass, the stag and all who were available, to plan his defence.

Meanwhile, the tom-tit was busy on his side enlisting the creatures of the air, including a large army of hornets, gnats, bees and flies.

As the time approached for the battle, the tom-tit sent out spies to ascertain who was to command the enemy forces. The gnat, who was by far the cleverest spy of them all, flew back and forth where the enemy troops were training. Finally locating the very place where the orders of the day were read out, he hid himself under a leaf on a nearby tree and listened carefully. He heard the bear call the fox to his side and say:

"Reynard, as you are the most cunning amongst us, you shall be our general and lead us into battle."

"I will signal," said the fox, "with my fine bushy tail, which resembles a plume of red feathers and gives me a warlike air. Now, remember, when you see me raise my tail, you may be sure that the battle is as good as won. You must charge the enemy and put them to rout. But if you see my tail droop, you will know that the battle is lost and you must run for your lives."

When the gnat had heard this, he flew back to the tom-tit to give him a full report.

At daybreak, on the day of the battle, the fox lead his army of beasts, advancing with such fearful sounds and beating of drums that the earth trembled.

From the other end of the wood, his majesty the tom-tit, surrounded by his troops, came flying along in warlike array, flapping and buzzing and beating the air. Both armies faced each other across a clearing. King Tom-Tit gave orders to a group of hornets that they should fly straight towards Reynard, and sting him about his tail with all of their might and main.

The battle began, and as the two armies met, the hornets, as instructed, flew straight for Reynard's tail and stung him ferociously. Startled and sore, he shook first one leg and then the other, but bravely held his tail aloft. At the second attack, he was forced to drop his tail momentarily, but as the hornets dived again, he could bear it no longer. He clapped his tail between his legs and ran for cover. When the other beasts saw this, they thought that all was lost and turned and ran for their lives, leaving the triumphant tom-tit and his army, masters of the field.

The tom-tit king and queen returned proudly to their children saying, "Now children, you can eat and drink, for victory is ours!"

But the young birds still refused. "No," they said, "not until Bruin has humbly begged our pardon for calling us base-born brats."

So the king flew back to the bear's den, and called, "Villain! I command you to come to my nest and humbly beg forgiveness from my dear children for your wicked insults. If you refuse, every bone in your wretched body shall be broken!"

The bear was terrified, and obediently did as he was told, after which, the little birds all sat down to a splendid meal which lasted long past their bedtime.